Tom, Katie and Friends
CARE

Ruth   Jason   Tom   Katie   Sita   Andy   Max

Eira Reeves and Shirley Pope

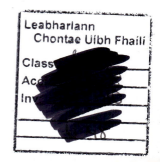

It was a lovely spring morning and the sun was shining. Jason and Andy were on their way to visit Katie.
"It's a pity Tom can't join us today," said Andy. "He's staying at home because he's feeling poorly."

"I'm looking forward to seeing Katie,"
said Jason. "Her mum said she would
like us to do something special today."
They were both excited.
"I wonder what we'll be doing," said Andy.
"I've no idea," replied Jason.

"Hello you two," said Katie's mum, Mrs Harris.
"It's so lovely to see you both."
Jason and Andy joined Katie at the table.
"Would you like a drink and some biscuits?"
asked Mrs Harris.
"Yes, please," they all replied.
Mrs Harris handed round the drinks
and biscuits.

"Thank you so much," said Andy.
"They're my favourite biscuits."
The three friends enjoyed eating
and chatting together.

"Well," said Mrs Harris, "I thought
we would do something different today.
I want you to help me plant some flower seeds."
"Ooooh," said Jason, laughing.
"I've never done that before!"
"Neither have I," said Andy,
"but it sounds like good fun!"
"Well," said Katie, boasting,
"I've planted lots and lots
of seeds before."

"Perhaps we can learn a little bit about caring for one another too," said Mrs Harris. "That's a funny way to learn about caring – by planting seeds," whispered Andy to Jason. They both giggled.
Andy carried a watering can,
Jason had some garden labels
and a pencil, and Katie carried
a fork and a trowel.

Mrs Harris walked ahead of them,
clutching some packets of seeds.
"Come on, everyone," said Mrs Harris.
"We have some work to do now.
Follow me!"

In the garden, Mrs Harris gave the packets of seeds to Katie, Andy and Jason.

"We're going to plant some sunflower seeds,"
said Mrs Harris, "and the plants
will grow **VERY TALL**."
"Bet mine will grow the tallest!" shouted Jason.
"No, bet **MINE** will!" yelled Andy.
"Jason and Andy," said Mrs Harris sternly,
"this is all about planting seeds and caring —
it's not a competition."

"First we need to dig up some of the weeds," said Mrs Harris. They all helped one another. It was quite hard. The weeds were tough and difficult to get out of the ground.

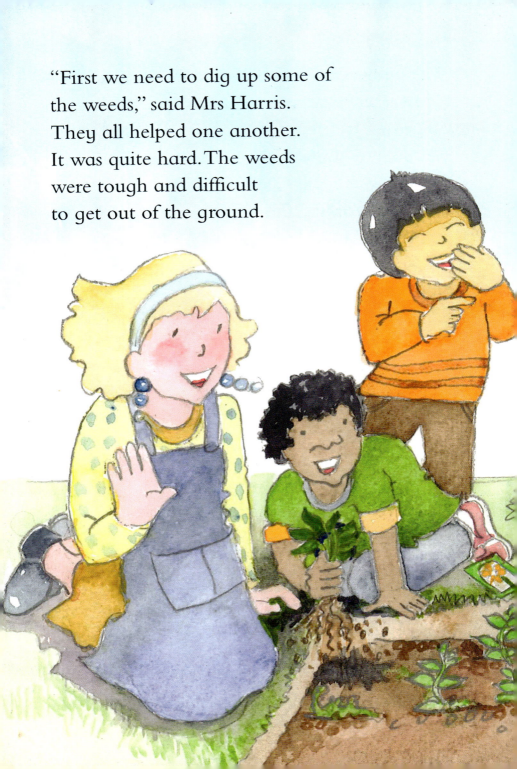

Katie pulled at one weed – but she pulled
too hard. Next moment she fell backwards
and lumps of earth flew into the air!
"Oh bother!" said Katie.
"I'm all covered in dirt!"
Everyone laughed.

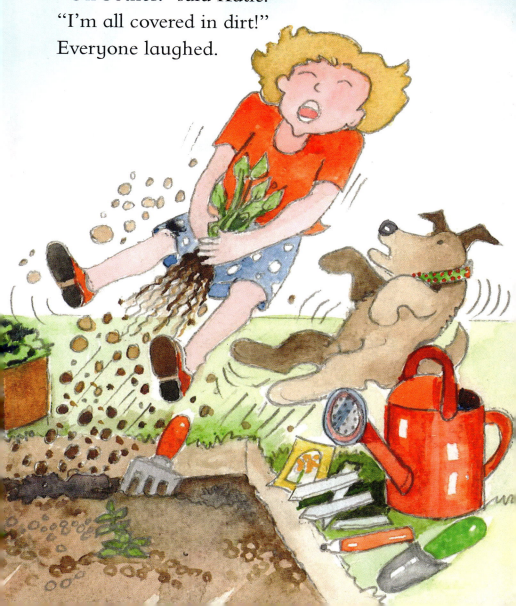

Andy was very busy.
He pulled out what he thought was a weed
"**OH NO!**" cried Mrs Harris, looking very cross.
"That's not a weed. It's one of my
lovely flowering plants!"

"Sorry, Mrs Harris," he said. "I don't have a garden so I don't know the difference between a plant and a weed!"
"Well," said Mrs Harris, "I hope you will learn very quickly."

One by one the seeds were planted
in the ground. Mrs Harris wrote
on the garden labels the word **SUNFLOWER**.
Then she asked Katie, Jason and Andy
to put labels in the ground where they
had planted their seeds.
"I'm enjoying today!" said Andy.
"I wonder how long it will take
for these plants to grow."

Jason thought his label made a nice aeroplane.
Mrs Harris told him off.

"Now," said Mrs Harris, "we must look after the seeds we have planted. They are very special – just like you. They will need to be watered every day so they grow into beautiful plants. Remember," she continued, "I want you to take care of each other's plants with lots of loving care."

"We will," said Jason, smiling.

Katie watered her seeds and
then she watered Jason's and Andy's seeds.
"That's kind of you, Katie," said Andy.
"Thank you."

"Looking after these plants is like looking after one another," said Mrs Harris.
"We need to take care of one another daily so our friendships will grow … just as the plants will grow when you care for them."
All three friends smiled and nodded at each other.

"It's a very important lesson to learn,
how to take care of one another,"
said Mrs Harris.
All three friends nodded again.

When the three friends had finished planting their seeds, Andy and Jason packed the garden tools away. They left the garden looking very tidy.

"Thank you for showing us how to plant seeds, Mrs Harris," said Jason. "I've enjoyed it so much."
"Thank you, too," said Andy, "for teaching us how to care for one another."
"I'm glad you learnt something new today," said Mrs Harris.
Jason and Andy waved goodbye to Katie and her mum.

CARE

**Interactive questions for the
teacher/parent and children**

★ Can you say what caring for someone is?

★ Have you ever had to care for someone?
If so, what did you do?

★ What care could you offer someone
you know today?

★ Has anyone ever cared for you?
If so, who were they and what did they do?

★ Name some ways in which you
could care for your family and friends.